ANIMALS ON THE EDGE

Sea Turtles' RACE to the SEA

A Cause and Effect Investigation

by Kathy Allen

Consultant:
Daniel Evans
Technology & Research Specialist
Sea Turtle Conservancy
Gainesville, Florida

CAPSTONE PRESS

Fact Finders are published by Capstone Press,
151 Good Counsel Drive, P.O. Box 669, Mankato, Minnesota 56002.
www.capstonepub.com

Library of Congress Cataloging-in-Publication Data
Allen, Kathy.
 Sea turtles' race to the sea : a cause and effect investigation / by Kathy Allen.
   p. cm. — (Fact finders. Animals on the edge)
 Summary: "Describes the sea turtle and its disappearing habitat"—Provided by publisher.
 ISBN 978-1-4296-5402-9 (library binding)
 1. Sea turtles—Effect of human beings on—Juvenile literature. 2. Sea turtles—Conservation—Juvenile
literature. 3. Endangered species—Juvenile literature. I. Title. II. Series.

 QL666.C536A46 2011
 597.92'8168—dc22   2010033003

Editorial Credits
Mari Bolte, editor; Ashlee Suker, designer; Marcie Spence, media researcher;
   Eric Manske, production specialist

Photo Credits
Ardea: Joanna Van Gruisen, 22, Valerie Taylor, 15; iStockphoto: PriamoMelo, 10, rontography, 8
(middle left); Minden Pictures: Gerry Ellis, 11, Jurgen Freund/NPL, 25, Mitsuaki Iwago, 7, 9, Norbert
Wu, 18, 19, Rebecca Hosking/FLPA, 14; Nature Picture Library: David Fleetham, 16; Peter Arnold:
Doug Perrine, 8 (bottom left), Martin Harvey, cover; Sea Turtle Conservancy/www.conserveturtles.org,
20, 21, 23; Shutterstock: amskad, 8 (top left), Anna-Lena Lewerenz, 28 (top), artcphotos, 13, CWB, 12,
Joe White, 8 (middle right), Lawrence Cruciana, 27, Lynsey Allen, 24, Matthew Cole, cover (shell),
Rich Carey, 4, 8 (middle left), 26, Robert Adrian Hillman, 28 (bottom); Visuals Unlimited: David
Fleetham, 17; Wikimedia: Bernard Gagnon, 8 (bottom right), Johntex, 8 (top right).

Printed in the United States of America in Stevens Point, Wisconsin.
092010   005934WZS11

TABLE OF CONTENTS

CHAPTER 1

Sea Turtles on the Edge

Sea turtles are one of the world's oldest creatures.

Somewhere in the Gulf of Mexico, a sea turtle pushes itself through warm coastal waters. Its large front limbs are flippers. The water flows quickly over its hard shell. Like all turtles, this creature is a **reptile** that breathes air. But it will never return to land. Sea turtles spend most of their lives in the sea.

reptile—a cold-blooded animal that breathes air

Sea turtles have been around for 150 million years. As one of the oldest animals on Earth, they are important creatures. Cultures around the world worship them. Divers and beach visitors love seeing them in their natural **habitat**. But recently sea turtles' habitat has changed.

Today sea turtles face new threats to their survival. Populations have decreased so much that there is a chance they will become extinct. What could have caused this? What could threaten an animal that has lived since the time of the dinosaurs?

The seven **species** of sea turtles are all large in size. Even the smallest species, Kemp's Ridley, weighs around 100 pounds (45.4 kilograms). The largest sea turtles can reach 2,000 pounds (907 kg). The shells of these giant turtles can be 5 feet (1.5 meters) long, although giants with 8-foot (2.4-m) shells have been reported. Each sea turtle species has its own diet. Some eat sea grass while others eat meat such as shrimp and crab. Sea turtles are good at finding food. They can see and smell very well underwater.

habitat—the place and natural conditions in which an animal lives
species—a group of animals with similar features

Sea Turtle Range

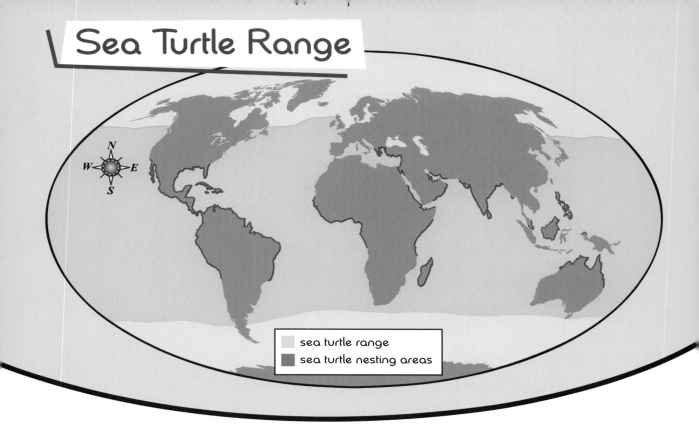

sea turtle range
sea turtle nesting areas

Sea turtles can be found in almost all the oceans around the world. They spend most of their time at sea. Adult females briefly return to land to lay eggs. They nest on warm, tropical beaches. Adults have been known to swim as far as 1,400 miles (2,253 kilometers) to reach their chosen nesting grounds.

Scientists don't know exactly how long sea turtles live. They believe a sea turtle can live as long as a human, about 70 to 80 years. There's a reason sea turtles live to such an old age. Once they become adults, sea turtles have few natural predators. Sea turtles are most at risk from predators when they are hatchlings.

In some areas, only one in 10,000 hatchlings reaches adulthood.

A Sea Turtle is Born

Sea turtles start their life on land. Under cover of night, female turtles lay between 80 and 160 eggs in the sand. After two months, hatchlings break through their shells and begin digging their way out. They usually break the nest's surface at night. Hatchlings use the bright horizon over the ocean to find the waterfront. Males, for the most part, never return to land. Decades later females return to the beach where they were born to lay their own eggs.

Kinds of Sea Turtles

- endangered
- threatened
- endangered and threatened
- vulnerable

Leatherback

Kemp's Ridley

Hawksbill

Loggerhead

Green

Olive Ridley

Flatback

Tiny sea turtle hatchlings are a food source for predators such as crabs and birds. Sea turtles have learned to survive despite these threats.

Sea turtles are **endangered** because of humans. From egg to hatchling to adult, human actions are a constant threat. Some of these threats, such as hunting, are easy to see. Others, such as habitat destruction, are less obvious, but no less deadly. Without action from **conservationists** and those who love animals, sea turtles are in danger. They could disappear from their warm ocean waters forever.

Predators are not the only threat to sea turtles' survival.

endangered—at risk of dying out
conservationist—someone involved with the protection of natural resources

WHAT HUMAN ACTIONS ARE HARMING SEA TURTLES?

CHAPTER 2

The Human Threat

Over hundreds, thousands, and millions of years, species go extinct. Extinction is a natural process that usually takes a long time. But today, many species are threatened by human actions. Sea turtles are one of these species.

Hundreds of thousands of sea turtles once swam in the ocean. Now they are threatened or endangered. Species are considered threatened if it's likely they will become endangered in the near future. Endangered species are those near extinction throughout most or all of their range. The flatback turtle is the only species of sea turtle that doesn't fall under these categories. Its range and nesting areas are in remote areas.

In 1503 Christopher Columbus named the Cayman Islands "Las Tortugas" because of the many sea turtles he saw there. Today only a fraction of the original turtle population remains.

Although illegal, nearly 1 million people eat turtle eggs or meat on a regular basis.

Some species have been hit harder than others. Between 80 and 90 percent of hawksbill sea turtles have vanished in the last 100 years. One of the biggest dangers to sea turtles is hunting. Turtles are hunted for their shells, meat, eggs, and skin. In some areas such as Central America and Asia, they are hunted for food or used in ceremonies. Their eggs are used for cooking, baking, and in medicines. Their shells are used to make jewelry and decorations. Killing sea turtles or taking their eggs is against the law in many countries.

One dog can dig up thousands of sea turtle eggs in one night.

Sea turtles face an even bigger threat as their habitats are destroyed. Sea turtles live in two habitats over their lifetime—beaches and oceans. They are born and travel as hatchlings on beaches. Crabs, birds, and even ants prey on sea turtle eggs and hatchlings. But now dogs and cats roam the beaches where their owners live. These animals also disturb sea turtle nests.

Raccoons, attracted to food left by humans, are common nighttime visitors. Raccoon populations have skyrocketed in beachside cities. These new predators live alongside human populations near the coast. In some areas, raccoons have been responsible for 100 percent of destroyed sea turtle nests.

The building of beach houses, stores, and sea walls also threatens nesting sites. Building on beaches can cause **erosion** and disturb the sand replacement that occurs naturally. Lighting from houses, stores, and streets confuse hatchlings that use the moon's light to find the sea.

Sea walls keep beaches from eroding. However, they also decrease the amount of space available to nesting sea turtles.

erosion—a slow wearing away of soil by water or wind

More than 100,000 marine animals die every year after getting tangled in plastic bags.

If a hatchling does make it to the ocean, new threats wait in the open waters. One threat is polluted ocean water. Around the world, chemicals from **fertilizers** flow into rivers that feed the oceans. Coral reefs that shelter turtles and other marine creatures are being destroyed by pollution. Oil spills, human waste, and litter also pollute the sea. Sea turtles have died eating tar and plastic bags that look like floating jellyfish.

Turtles also face the danger of fishing nets used to catch shrimp and other fish. Thousands of sea turtles die each year by getting caught in these nets and drowning.

fertilizer—a substance used to make crops grow better

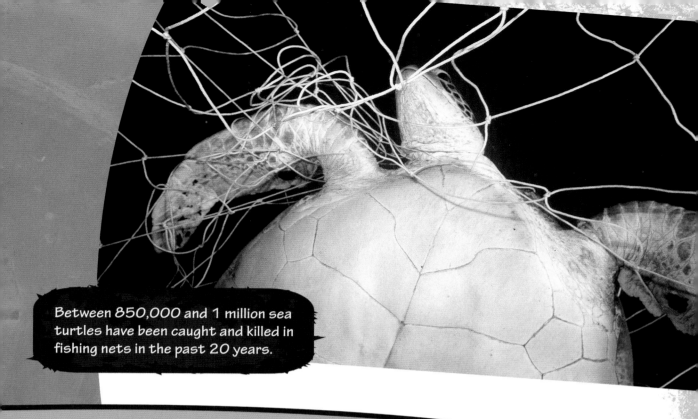

Between 850,000 and 1 million sea turtles have been caught and killed in fishing nets in the past 20 years.

Amazing Migrations

Throughout their lives, sea turtles follow their food. They migrate through the world's oceans looking for things to eat. A loggerhead turtle in the Pacific Ocean covers one-third of the entire planet in its migration. In 2008 a leatherback turtle set a new record for the longest migration. Scientists tracked the female's 12,744-mile (20,509-km) Pacific journey as she swam from Papua, Indonesia, to the U.S. state of Oregon.

Growths caused by FP can cause permanent blindness.

Hunting and habitat destruction are clearly caused by humans. But scientists aren't sure what's causing a new disease that threatens sea turtles. Commonly called FP, this disease causes tumorlike growths to appear on the outside and inside of a turtle's body. Turtles with severe FP are also at high risk for infection from worms. Others have developed growths in their throat. The growths prevent the throat from closing. This opening allows food and seawater to enter the turtles' lungs, causing them to choke and drown.

The disease has now been found in most kinds of sea turtles. Some growths are so large the sea turtle cannot swim or eat. No one knows for sure what causes FP, or how to cure it. Scientists do know that FP is more common in turtles that live near areas with many people. The sudden rise of the disease leads some to believe that pollution is to blame.

Green turtles (pictured) and loggerheads have been hit the hardest by FP.

WHAT CAN BE DONE TO HELP SEA TURTLES?

CHAPTER 3
Saving the Sea Turtle

Sea turtles around the world are near extinction. Species found in the United States are protected under the Endangered Species Act. This act works to keep endangered species and their habitats healthy. All sea turtles are protected under the conservation treaty known as CITES. This treaty includes 172 countries that have banned the selling and trading of sea turtles and their products.

People are becoming more aware of the sea turtle and the problems it faces.

TURTLE XING

Many states and cities have passed laws to protect sea turtles. Some limit lighting near nesting sites that might confuse young turtles. Sometimes conservationists move sea turtle eggs to hatcheries. The hatchlings are later released into the wild. Others protect sea turtles in the ocean by following laws against polluting ocean waters. Fishers on shrimp boats protect sea turtles with a Turtle Exclusion Device (TED). This trap door allows sea turtles to escape from fishing nets.

The first step to helping sea turtles is understanding them. Because they live most of their lives in the ocean, sea turtles are not easy to study. That's why scientists don't know exactly how long a sea turtle lives. But scientists study nesting sites every summer. At many nesting sites, scientists attach flipper tags to adult turtles. These tags track turtles over time. Some are tracked by satellite and can be followed on the Internet. Tracking gives scientists information about how sea turtles live.

Tracking tags monitor sea turtles for periods of six months to a year.

DO NOT DISTURB
SEA TURTLE
NEST
VIOLATORS SUBJECT
TO FINES AND
IMPRISONMENT

Scientists mark sea turtle nests and record information such as location, hatching time, and number of hatched eggs.

Conservationists also share information about sea turtles. They work to educate people around the world about turtles. Sea turtles cross many borders and travel much of the world in their lives. Sharing information helps scientists learn more about sea turtles.

Even something as simple as reading a book about sea turtles can help them. The more people understand sea turtles, the more they know how to protect them. But there's more you can do than read. Sea turtles need dark, quiet beaches to nest. People who live near sea turtle nesting sites can help by not picking up eggs or hatchlings. They should also avoid shining flashlights on beaches at night during the nesting season.

Some beaches are protected areas. These areas help ensure sea turtle hatchlings are safe as they make their way to the ocean.

The tracks of nesting turtles should be left alone. Scientists use those tracks to mark nest sites. Some cities even have nesting patrols. These patrols find and record nesting sites. Knowing where the sites are helps researchers decide whether people should be kept away. Nesting sea turtles, their eggs, and their hatchlings are safest when they are away from people.

Sea turtle tracks are used by researchers to discover the number of new nests.

CHAPTER 4

A Piece of the Puzzle

Why work so hard to save sea turtles? Sea turtles are part of an **ecosystem**. Animals and plants in an ecosystem rely on each other and their habitat to live. When one piece of that natural puzzle is broken, it affects all the other parts. For example, sea turtle eggs provide **nutrients** for plants. In one area in Florida, sea turtles lay more than 150,000 pounds (68,039 kg) of eggs. Not all of these will hatch. Plants in the area grow stronger on the nutrients in the unhatched eggs and shells. The plants' roots slow erosion and keep beaches stable.

Sand beaches receive very few nutrients throughout the year. Sea turtle eggs are important to the beach ecosystem.

Sea turtles are a small but important part of the beach ecosystem.

Humans are also a part of this ecosystem. The health of a beach is important to people who live there. Sea turtles are symbols of that health. They are signs that a beach is doing well. Turtles help coastal habitats thrive by eating sea grasses and laying their eggs in the sand. In turn, the beach provides a safe place for turtles to nest. Changes in sea turtle numbers or their health tells us when something might be wrong with their habitat.

ecosystem—animals and plants that interact with their environment
nutrient—a substance needed by a living thing to stay healthy

Sea Turtles and Sea Grass

Sea turtles are one of the few animals that eat sea grass. Sea grass is similar to the grass in your lawn, except that it grows on the sea floor. Sea turtles eat this grass, which keeps the area healthy and growing. Many animals breed and develop in sea grass beds, including sea turtles. There are fewer sea grass beds today than there were 20 years ago. Researchers think this is because there are fewer sea turtles.

An adult green sea turtle can eat 4.4 pounds (2 kg) of sea grass every day.

The future of the sea turtle depends on humans.

But sea turtles are important for more than just their ecosystem. Sea turtles are important symbols in the religions and myths of people who live on the coast. Humans are fascinated by these ancient, long-lived animals. Sea turtles are world-travelling, mysterious creatures. They are also a flagship species.

Because sea turtles are so loved, they create interest in saving habitats where many other animals and plants live. Sea turtles have also become tourist draws. These animal lovers want to learn about the ocean. Learning about sea turtles is one way to ensure that these ancient creatures don't disappear.

Sea Turtles' Ecosystems

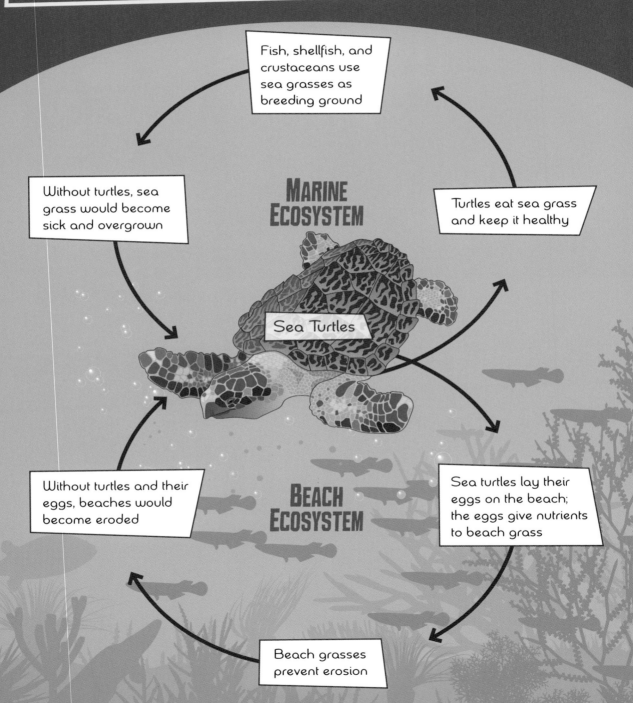

Fish, shellfish, and crustaceans use sea grasses as breeding ground

Without turtles, sea grass would become sick and overgrown

MARINE ECOSYSTEM

Turtles eat sea grass and keep it healthy

Sea Turtles

Without turtles and their eggs, beaches would become eroded

BEACH ECOSYSTEM

Sea turtles lay their eggs on the beach; the eggs give nutrients to beach grass

Beach grasses prevent erosion

Resources To Help Sea Turtles

Sea Turtle Conservancy

Founded in 1959, the Sea Turtle Conservancy was the first conservation program for sea turtles. The organization spreads the word about the risks sea turtles face. Working with scientists, conservationists, and educators, the Sea Turtle Conservancy works to save sea turtles from extinction.

Defenders of Wildlife

Defenders of Wildlife has been protecting animals at risk since 1947. Today the organization has more than 50,000 members worldwide. This group works to protect both wildlife and the land they live on.

World Wildlife Fund

As the world's leading conservation organization, the World Wildlife Fund encourages people to take action at every level—local and global Located in 100 countries, the WWF works to educate people about the world around them.

Index